W9-CFQ-546

11/13

DATE DUE

HIGHSMITH 45230

PERSONAL FREEDOM & CIVIC DUTY™

UNDERSTANDING THE
RULE OF LAW
NO ONE IS ABOVE THE LAW

G.S. PRENTZAS

ROSEN
PUBLISHING®

New York

Published in 2014 by The Rosen Publishing Group, Inc.
29 East 21st Street, New York, NY 10010

First Edition

Library of Congress Cataloging-in-Publication Data

Prentzas, G. S.
Understanding the rule of law: no one is above the law/G. S.
Prentzas.
    p. cm.—(Personal freedom & civic duty)
Includes bibliographical references and index.
ISBN 978-1-4488-9464-2 (library binding)
1. Rule of law—United States. I. Title.
KF382.P74 2013
340'.11—dc23

2012040027

Manufactured in the United States of America

CPSIA Compliance Information: Batch #S13YA: For further information, contact Rosen Publishing, New York,
New York, at 1-800-237-9932.

CONTENTS

INTRODUCTION

A fter officially gaining independence from Great Britain in 1783, the United States faced many challenges. The young nation needed to repair damages caused by the American Revolution and build a stronger economy. It had to develop relationships with the other nations of the world. It also needed to strengthen its central government.

Above: The Constitution, Declaration of Independence, and Bill of Rights are under tight security at the National Archives in Washington, D.C., where they are kept.

In May 1787, delegates from all of the thirteen states except for Rhode Island sent delegates to the Constitutional Convention in Philadelphia. The delegates met to discuss creating a stronger federal government. The Articles of Confederation had set up the first U.S. government in 1777. This agreement between the states intentionally created a weak federal government to conduct the war and to handle a few minor functions. The federal government had no power to tax citizens, so it could not raise money to carry out its duties. The Articles of Confederation also provided no process for the central government to resolve disputes between the states.

After much discussion and debate, the delegates drafted a document that provided the framework for a new federal government. On September 17, they voted to adopt the U.S. Constitution. The convention then presented the Constitution to the states for ratification, or approval.

While still considering whether to approve the Constitution, several states demanded that a list of rights be added to the document. These amendments would prevent the central government from denying basic rights to citizens. In September 1789, the first U.S. Congress proposed twelve amendments to the Constitution. By January 1791, the legislatures of all thirteen states had voted to accept the Constitution and ten of the twelve proposed amendments.

The U.S. Constitution separates the powers of the central governmental into three different branches—legislative, executive, and judiciary. To prevent one person or a group from becoming too powerful, the Constitution requires that the three branches cooperate. It provides methods for each branch to limit the power of the other two branches. The Constitution also recognizes the important role of the states. It gives the federal government authority over certain areas. The states have authority over all other areas.

The first three sections of the Constitution outline the three federal branches of government. Article I sets up a federal legislative branch, known as Congress. The legislative branch has two chambers, the House of Representatives and the Senate. Article I describes the terms and qualifications for representatives and senators. It also specifies the governmental powers of Congress. Article II establishes the executive branch. This branch includes the office of the president and vice president, as well as the Department of State and other federal departments and agencies. Article II sets the qualifications for the presidents and outlines the powers of the executive branch. Article III establishes the federal judiciary. It specifies the types of cases federal courts can hear.

The other five articles of the Constitution cover such issues as the process for the states to ratify the Constitution and the process for admitting new states to the Union. Article V details how the Constitution may be amended, or changed. A proposed constitutional amendment must be approved by a two-thirds vote of both the House of Representatives and the Senate. Then the legislatures of at least three-quarters of the states must approve the amendment for it to become part of the Constitution.

The first ten amendments to the Constitution are known as the Bill of Rights. They became part of the Constitution at the same time in 1791. These ten amendments protect the basic rights of U.S. citizens. For example, the First Amendment prohibits Congress from passing any law that restricts a person's right to practice any religion or to limit speech. Other amendments protect a wide range of individual rights, from gun ownership to the right of a jury trial in federal cases.

The preamble, or introduction, to the Constitution declares that the government in the United States is created by and subject to the will of its citizens. This theory of government is known as popular sovereignty. At all levels of government, voters elect people to government offices. These officials serve the interests of everyone. Once in office, elected government officials, as well as appointees, must enforce the law equally. Most important, the laws also apply equally to government officials. Under the legal and political structure created by the Constitution, no one person is above the law. This broad concept that laws apply to everyone and protect the rights of individuals is known as the rule of law. The rule of law is central to understanding the role of government in the United States and the personal freedoms of its citizens.

The rule of law is a set of laws and legal procedures that make certain no one is above the law. That includes individuals, groups, political leaders, and government officials. Many countries have adopted the rule of law. In these countries, kings, presidents, and other government officials are not allowed to exercise their authority beyond the limits set by law. The rule of law helps protect societies and individuals from government actions that are based only on an official's personal wishes. The laws of the nation are supreme. They apply equally to all citizens and government officials.

Throughout history, the rule of law has been a key factor in establishing and maintaining social order. The Greek philosopher Aristotle (384–322 BCE) observed that the rule of law is better than the rule of an individual. In *Politics: A Treatise on Government*, Aristotle wrote, "It is more proper that law should govern than any one of the citizens: upon the same principle, if it is advantageous to place the supreme power in some particular persons, they should be appointed to be only guardians, and the servants

Greek philosopher Aristotle endorsed the rule of law in his writings on politics and government.

of the laws." The rule of law arose as a way to end the absolute power of monarchs and dictators without sacrificing social order.

The rule of law established that the law—rather than desires of an absolute ruler or powerful, wealthy individuals—would serve as the foundation of society. The rule of law requires that all government officials base their actions and decisions on established laws and rules. They must also enforce laws by following established procedural steps known as due process. When everyone, including government officials, must follow a nation's laws, people are less likely to suffer as a result of an arbitrary decision by a government official.

BASIC PRINCIPLES

Legal systems based on the rule of law share a set of basic principles. When these principles are present, a legal system is more likely to produce fair results and a stable society.

Laws Are Stable and Public

Under the rule of law, a nation's laws and legal procedures are adopted by following an established legislative process. Legislative power is exercised primarily by a legislature. The power to enforce laws resides primarily in an executive branch. The legislature can delegate some rule-making authority to the nation's executive branch. However, laws place restrictions on the ability of the executive branch to make laws. The nation's laws also set up a method of judicial review. The nation's judiciary has the power to review laws to make sure they are valid under the laws of the nation. For example, a court may invalidate a law preventing people from practicing their religion, as forbidding freedom of religion violates the nation's constitution.

The rule of law requires that a nation's laws and procedures be stable. Stable laws help people understand the boundaries of the law. A judicial system that follows legal precedents helps maintain stable laws. Judicial precedents are decisions in court cases that serve as a model for later cases. By adopting the reasoning of courts that heard earlier similar cases, judges make a nation's laws clearer and more predictable.

A nation's laws should be known to citizens. By announcing its laws and regulations publicly, a government gives citizens notice of what is expected of them. When a citizen breaks a law, the government can use its power to charge the person with a violation of the law. When people know how government power will be used, they can avoid breaking the law. For example, imagine that a nation's laws give citizens the freedom to protest peacefully against the government. Protesters know that they can voice their

DUE PROCESS AND EQUAL PROTECTION

Due process and equal protection are important elements of the rule of law. In the United States, the Fifth Amendment to the U.S. Constitution states, "No person shall be . . . deprived of life, liberty, or property, without due process of law." Due process means that the procedures in courts and other legal proceedings must respect the rights of individuals. The Fourteenth Amendment requires the states to provide every person "the equal protection of the laws." Equal protection means that laws must treat an individual in the same manner as others in similar conditions and circumstances.

political opinions publicly without consequence. In contrast, in a country that has a king with absolute power and no rule of law, the king might have protesters arrested because he doesn't like what they are saying. There may be no law forbidding protests. Yet the king has the power to order the arrest of protesters anyway. Nothing limits the king's actions. The people are subject to his wishes.

Citizens Have Access to a Justice System

Under the rule of law, a government provides citizens with access to a system of justice. The judiciary system is independent of the legislative and executive

A witness *(center)* prepares to testify during a murder trial in a U.S. courtroom. Fair and open trials are an important part of the rule of law.

branches. It helps protect citizens from arbitrary government power. The justice system also protects citizens from harms caused by other people. It outlaws murder, robbery, and similar crimes. It also protects people from corporations and other groups by outlawing deceptive advertising, air pollution, and other harmful things. The judiciary system should have enough judges, staff, and lawyers to handle cases effectively.

Legal Procedures Are Fair

For the rule of law to function, judicial and law enforcement procedures must treat everyone in the same manner. Individuals accused of a crime or other violations of the law are informed of the charges against them. They have the right to legal counsel. They also have the right to have their case heard by an unbiased judge or jury. Judges must avoid political influence when deciding cases. Accused people have the right to present evidence and arguments to prove their innocence. They also have the right to have the decision in their case based only on the evidence produced at the trial or hearing.

Government Officials Are Held Accountable

Under the rule of law, a nation's laws describe how government officials must exercise their powers. Laws place limits on the powers of government officials. The law is always supreme. All government officials—kings, presidents,

A driver hands her license to a police officer during a traffic stop. Law enforcement officers have the power to enforce local and national laws, but they must also follow the law in carrying out their official duties.

senators, judges, law enforcement officers—are subject to the law.

Laws and procedures restrict how much discretion government officials have. In theory, the rule of law requires government officials to follow laws and procedures precisely. In practice, national laws give government officials some room to make their own decisions. For example, police officers have discretion when using their authority to issue speeding tickets. An officer may decide not to stop a driver going slightly over the speed limit but later ticket a driver going much faster. The rule of law encourages public officials to use sound judgment when using their discretion. The discretionary decisions of government officials must be based on good reasons rather than personal whim.

Open Government

The rule of law promotes government transparency and openness. Transparency means that the law requires government officials to provide the public with information about what they are doing. By holding legislative debates, trials, and government meetings in public, governments enable citizens to observe their actions. By publishing information about their work, government agencies let citizens know about the decisions and actions of government officials.

Transparency helps deter political corruption. When the public can see what the government is doing, it makes it less likely that government officials will act in their own interest rather than in the public interest. For example, government officials are less likely to accept bribes if their actions are a part of the public record. Openness means that citizens have a chance to participate in government. By monitoring government actions and decisions, people can provide feedback to politicians and government officials. They can also hold politicians and officials accountable for their actions.

Legal Protections

The rule of law provides legal protections to individuals. It prevents government officials from harming people by acting or making decisions outside of the law. For example, laws prevent police officers from obtaining criminal confessions by force. The rule of law also helps guarantee fundamental rights. Fundamental rights include freedom of speech, freedom of religion, and the right to legal counsel. If a government official or a new law violates or restricts an individual's fundamental rights, the person can ask the judiciary system to uphold his or her rights.

The rule of law promotes effective criminal justice by establishing procedures that help ensure

Demonstrators march before the Democratic National Convention to call attention to the impact of corporate money on politics and government.

equal treatment of suspects and produce fair trials. It also provides people with access to civil courts. An individual who is harmed by another person or corporation may file a lawsuit seeking to be compensated for his or her losses.

Social Benefits

The rule of law provides the foundation for social order and economic security. It informs citizens about what conduct is legal and what conduct will not be tolerated. It provides businesses and consumers with rules of fair commercial conduct. For example, laws prevent businesses from using false or deceptive claims in their advertisements. These laws protect both consumers and other businesses.

In countries that operate under the rule of law, people have greater confidence in conducting their lives. They can buy property, start businesses, and make other plans for the future. Because the rule of law limits the power of government, individuals are not subject to arbitrary government actions. It gives them the freedom to pursue any legal activity they want.

THE RULE OF LAW AND JUSTICE

The rule of law promotes justice but does not ensure it. The existence of the rule of law does not depend on the content of laws. The rule of law requires only that no person is above the law and that government procedures are fair. A country can operate within the rule of law and still be cruel and oppressive. Its legislature can pass laws that are unreasonable or severe. Government officials can enforce laws harshly while staying within the boundaries of their legal authority.

Even in the fairest legal systems, unfair results are possible. The rule of law merely requires the legal system to follow established procedures in each case. For example, an innocent defendant in a criminal case may go through a fair judicial process and be found guilty. Likewise, a defendant who committed a crime may avoid conviction.

The rule of law also does not guarantee equal outcomes in life. Laws and other rules help ensure that a society provides a level playing field for all members of society. Everyone is subject to the same laws and

A lawyer questions a witness. The rule of law establishes fair judicial procedures but does not guarantee a correct verdict in trials.

has a fair chance to pursue their goals in life. Based on skill, hard work, or good fortune, however, some individuals will produce better results. Inequities in education, wealth, and status will occur. The rule of law helps lower the chance of unfair outcomes. For example, in the United States, federal and state laws prohibit employers from discriminating on the basis of race, religion, sex, age, national origin, or physical disability. Antidiscrimination laws give everyone a fair opportunity to compete for jobs on the basis of their qualifications.

THE UNITED STATES AND THE RULE OF LAW

The rule of law was a central idea in the founding of the United States. The patriots who led the fight for independence from Great Britain had lived under the iron rule of a king. American colonists did not have the right to elect legislators to represent their interests in Parliament, Great Britain's legislature. Parliament approved taxes and passed other laws that many colonists felt treated them unfairly.

American colonists launched a revolution against Great Britain to escape the tyranny of absolute power. They lived in a society in which decisions were made by a faraway king and legislature. Many key decisions involving the colonies had been based on the desires of King George III or colonial officials appointed by him. George had allowed colonial officials and others to act outside existing law in the colonies. Colonists had no way to ensure that decisions affecting their lives would be made fairly.

The goal of the American Revolution was to get rid of the arbitrary will of a king. In its place, the people of the United States would install a new political and legal system. In this system, the law would apply equally to everyone—no matter how rich or powerful.

In 1776, Thomas Paine published *Common Sense* to persuade reluctant colonists to join the rebellion. In this pamphlet, Paine presented arguments for why the American colonies should break away from Great Britain. He also discussed how the new country would be governed. Paine wrote, "In America THE LAW IS KING. For as in absolute governments the King is the law, so in free countries the law ought to be King, and there ought to be no other." Like Paine, many leaders of the American Revolution believed that the law, not the judgment of an absolute ruler, should be the cornerstone of government. Inequalities in wealth, power, and prestige would exist in the new society. The law, however, would not treat any citizen differently.

The founders—George Washington, John Adams, Thomas Jefferson, James Madison, and

COMMON SENSE;

ADDRESSED TO THE

INHABITANTS

OF

AMERICA,

On the following interesting

SUBJECTS.

I. Of the Origin and Design of Government in general, with concise Remarks on the English Constitution.

II. Of Monarchy and Hereditary Succession.

III. Thoughts on the present State of American Affairs.

IV. Of the present Ability of America, with some miscellaneous Reflections.

Man knows no Master save creating HEAVEN,
Or those whom choice and common good ordain.

THOMSON.

Prin

Common Sense was one of the most important documents in the founding of the United States. In this essay, Thomas Paine made the case for creating a new nation based on the rule of law.

others—believed that the rule of law was the most effective tool to prevent government from becoming too powerful. They recognized that any nation's political legal system gave government officials tremendous powers. The government could take away the property and freedoms of an individual. It could even execute people for certain crimes. The founders worried that a powerful centralized government would eventually adopt the same arbitrary methods used by King George and other monarchs. In 1780, John Adams summarized the role the rule of law would play in the new nation. He wrote that the United States would be "an Empire of laws and not men."

In creating the United States, the founders of the nation wanted to avoid giving government officials the power to make arbitrary decisions. They chose to establish a society in which government decisions were made by officials following a set of laws and procedures. They wanted to reduce the discretion of government officials in making major decisions. Having experienced the tyranny of a king, these founders were dedicated to the idea of making law superior to the will of individuals.

To ensure that future generations would enjoy the benefits of a society governed by the rule of law, the founders wrote a document that defined the powers of government. The U.S. Constitution created a republic in which governmental power was divided between the federal government and the governments of the states. It separated the federal government into three branches. It assigned specific powers to each of these branches. It also gave each branch the ability to limit the power of the other two branches.

The founders set up a system of government that they hoped would prevent government officials from making decisions beyond their official authority. They incorporated the concept of equal protection of the law to ensure that no person was above the law. They wanted to ensure that future generations would be free from government tyranny.

Historians and legal scholars trace the origins of the rule of law in the United States back to the nation's colonial period. Spain established the first permanent European settlement in North America in 1595. A century earlier, Spain's King Ferdinand and Queen Isabella had hired Italian explorer Christopher Columbus to discover a western sailing route to Asia. His four voyages to the Americas between 1492 and 1503 had failed in that mission. But his stories of lands and peoples previously unknown to Europeans ignited Spain's interest in setting up colonies in the Americas.

Starting in 1500, Spain set up colonies in Cuba and other Caribbean islands, Central and South America, and present-day Mexico and Florida. Other European countries eventually joined Spain in colonizing the New World. By the early 1600s, France had successfully established colonies in what is now Canada. Holland established a colony in North America that stretched along the Hudson River in present-day New York. Sweden set up a small colony along the Delaware River.

THE BRITISH COLONIES

England established its first successful North American colony in 1607. Jamestown, located in present-day Virginia, started with about one hundred colonists. As England became a more powerful nation, it expanded its territory in North America. It seized control of the Dutch and Swedish colonies in the Middle Atlantic. By 1752, Great Britain's thirteen North American colonies stretched from what is now Maine to present-day Georgia.

About half of the original thirteen colonies were founded as colonies belonging to Great Britain. In each of these colonies, Great Britain's monarch appointed a governor to oversee the colony. In some colonies, the

This painting depicts Jamestown, Great Britain's first permanent settlement in what is now the United States. Great Britain's North American colony soon stretched along the Atlantic coastline.

governor created a legislature. The governor, who worked for the king, had the final say in all legal and political matters. Colonists had limited input in how their colonies were operated. The colonists had no representation in Parliament, Great Britain's legislature. They also had no control over selecting their governors or other colonial officials. These officials had almost absolute authority to manage the colonies' governments. They enforced British laws and regulations. Judges in colonial courts followed British laws when deciding cases.

Six colonies did not start out as royal colonies belonging directly to Great Britain. English monarchs had given a person or a company ownership of the colonies of Connecticut, Maryland, Massachusetts, New Jersey, Pennsylvania, and Rhode Island. For example, in 1681, King Charles II gave William Penn the exclusive right to settle a large area of North America. This territory is now known as Pennsylvania and Delaware. In each of these six colonies, its owner appointed a governor and other officials to oversee the colony. Several of the owners also set up a legislature and courts to govern the colony. These colonies were expensive to operate. Their owners eventually could not afford them. All six colony owners transferred their ownership rights to Great Britain.

As English settlers began pouring into the North American colonies, the relationship between colonists and native groups soured. Throughout the colonies, English settlers began intruding on Indian territories. Indian raids on colonial settlements became more frequent. In response to demands by colonists for protection, Great Britain sent more soldiers to the colonies. These soldiers were stationed in villages throughout British North America to defend colonists.

The colonists also faced threats from nearby French colonies. Great Britain and France tried to expand their North American territories. The two countries fought four wars between 1689 and 1763. The French and Indian War (1754–1763) was the final clash between the two European powers. British soldiers and colonists, along with their Indian allies, fought against French soldiers and settlers and their Indian allies. A British victory in the Battle of Quebec in 1759 was the decisive battle in the French and Indian War. In the treaty ending the war, France gave England most of its territories in North America.

TENSIONS RISE

Although Great Britain won the French and Indian War, all was not well in the British colonies. Tensions between colonists and colonial officials began to grow. The French and Indian War had cost Great Britain a lot of money. The end of hostilities with France did not end Indian attacks on colonial villages and settlers. Great Britain needed to pay for the high costs of the war. It also had to pay soldiers to defend its colonies against Indian attacks. Parliament passed several laws that required colonists to pay much higher taxes. The new taxes angered many colonists. The colonies had no legislators representing them in Parliament. British officials pointed out that Parliament was only making the colonists pay for their own protection.

In 1765, Parliament passed the Stamp Act to raise money. It required that all legal papers, newspapers, and other types of documents in the colonies receive an official stamp. Each stamp required a payment. The payment varied depending on the type of document. Many colonists felt that because they had no representatives in Parliament, they were being unfairly taxed. "No taxation without representation" became a popular slogan for colonists. They wanted a voice in how their colonies were governed. Some colonists began demanding representatives in Parliament. Others talked about

This painting shows American colonists, dressed as Native Americans, throwing crates of tea overboard into Boston Harbor. The colonists were protesting a

independence from Great Britain. In 1770, British troops fired into a hostile crowd in Boston. They killed five colonists. In 1773, Parliament imposed a new tax on tea in the colonies. A group of colonists protested against this tax. They destroyed British tea shipments in Boston's harbor. This event became known as the Boston Tea Party.

Parliament responded to the growing unrest in the colonies. It passed the Coercive Acts in 1774. The British navy closed down Boston's harbor. They told colonists that shipping would resume only when the colonies paid for the destroyed tea. Parliament also passed laws that enabled British commanders to house soldiers in buildings owned by colonists. Tensions between colonists and British officials grew. More colonists began calling for independence from Great Britain. They argued that Parliament had denied them basic rights. They were also subject to the unfair orders of governors and other British colonial officials. However, many other colonists remained loyal to England. Some wealthy businessmen did not want to risk their businesses. They made money by trading with Great Britain. Several colonies relied heavily on money from Parliament and supplies from Great Britain. Many colonists worried that the colonies would be unable to protect themselves from Indian attacks if the British troops left.

The First Continental Congress

In the fall of 1774, the legislatures of twelve colonies sent representatives to Philadelphia. (Georgia did not send any delegates.) The delegates to the First Continental Congress discussed how colonists should respond to the Coercive Acts and other laws. They planned a boycott to ask colonists to stop buying British goods. The delegates also recommended that all of the colonies form militias to defend themselves from British troops. They drafted a letter to Parliament. The letter asked the British legislature to cancel the Coercive Acts. Finally, the delegates agreed to meet again if the Coercive Acts remained in force. During the two months that the delegates met, there was little talk of independence. When Parliament received the petition from the First Continental Congress, it ignored the colonists' requests.

The Revolution Begins

The disagreements between the colonies and the British eventually erupted into armed conflict. In April 1775, Major General Thomas Gage, the British military commander in Boston, sent seven hundred soldiers to nearby Concord. Their mission was to arrest John Adams and other leaders of the growing independence movement. Gage also ordered his troops to seize any weapons they found. British soldiers marched toward Concord. They encountered a group of militiamen in the village of Lexington. The militiamen were citizens who armed themselves to resist British rule. The two sides exchanged musket fire. Eight militiamen were killed. Ten were wounded. The British troops continued marching. In Concord, they could not find any of the patriot leaders. They were able to destroy some weapons. A large group of militiamen had retreated when British troops entered Concord. When the militiamen saw that the British had set fire to the courthouse and black-smith shop, they confronted the soldiers. Gunfire was exchanged, resulting in

This painting shows minutemen in Lexington, Massachusetts, firing at British soldiers. The Battle of Lexington and Concord was the first skirmish in the American Revolution.

several deaths on both sides. The British troops retreated. The militiamen were waiting for them. They took cover behind trees and stone walls along the road to Boston. The militiamen peppered the British troops with musket fire. In total, the colonists killed twenty British soldiers and wounded about two hundred more.

The Battle of Lexington and Concord motivated colonists who wanted independence from Great Britain to call for another meeting. On May 10, 1775, sixty-five delegates from twelve colonies met in Philadelphia. (Georgia's delegates joined the meeting in July.) Many of the delegates to the Second Continental Congress still sought a peaceful solution

THE VIRGINIA DECLARATION OF RIGHTS

In May 1776, delegates at the Virginia Convention voted to declare the colonies independent of Great Britain. They also agreed to create a declaration of rights. George Mason drafted a document known as the Virginia Declaration of Rights.

The first two sections of the declaration proclaimed that all people have equal rights and that governments receive their power from citizens. One section provided for separation of powers in government. Another gave civilians, not military officers, control of the military. The declaration also guaranteed religious liberty, property rights, and freedom of the press. It prohibited unreasonable search and seizures and cruel and unusual punishments. The Virginia Declaration served as a model for the Declaration of Independence and the Bill of Rights.

to the conflict. They remained loyal to England. They tried to stop talk of independence.

The Second Continental Congress drafted another letter. It became known as the Olive Branch Petition. The petition asked King George III to resolve the conflict between the colonies and Parliament. William Penn carried the petition to London. The British monarch refused to see Penn or accept the colonists' petition. On August 23, 1775, King George III officially declared the American colonies to be in rebellion. He ordered British military officers and government officials to take measures to end the uprising.

A New Nation

The delegates to the Second Continental Congress had tried to find a peaceful solution to the conflict. They had also prepared for war. The delegates established the Continental army. They selected forty-three-year-old George Washington as its commander. As both sides prepared for war, the Second Continental Congress selected Thomas Jefferson to write a document. It would declare the thirteen colonies' independence from Great Britain. Some revisions were made to Jefferson's draft. The final document was presented to the Congress. On July 4, 1776, the delegates voted to approve the adoption of the Declaration of Independence. On August 2, fifty-six delegates signed the document.

A researcher views a scan of Thomas Jefferson's handwritten draft of the Declaration of Independence. The document explained why the colonies sought independence and announced the basic principles upon which the United States would be based.

The Declaration of Independence starts by proclaiming that "all men are created equal" and that they have rights that cannot be taken away. These basic rights include "life, liberty, and the pursuit of happiness." The declaration goes on to describe the various actions of Parliament and King George III that the delegates considered unjust and unacceptable. The document declared that the thirteen colonies are "Free and Independent States." It ended by proclaiming "all political connection between them and the State of Great Britain is . . . totally dissolved."

The Declaration of Independence includes a basic element that continues to support the rule of law in the United States. It states that governments get their powers "from the consent of the governed." It asserts that people have the right to change or abolish a government that treats its citizens unfairly and unjustly.

A New Country

The early years of the American Revolution went poorly for the Continental army. The patriots, however, eventually turned the war in their favor. In October 1791, British commander Charles Cornwallis surrendered at Yorktown, Virginia. Cornwallis's troops boarded ships and returned to Great Britain. The departure of British troops brought an end to the America Revolution. In September 1783, the United States and Great Britain signed the Treaty of Paris. The treaty officially ended the war. Great Britain agreed to recognize the United States as an independent country.

THE DEVELOPMENT OF THE RULE OF LAW

The Constitution is the primary source of the rule of law in the United States. It divides the powers of the federal government into three separate branches. The framers of the Constitution set up a political structure to make sure that no one branch would became too powerful. This structure, known as checks and balances, gives each branch specific ways to limit the power of the other two branches. Throughout U.S. history, the three branches have clashed over issues involving checks and balances. The scope of each branch's power, as well as the ways in which branches can control the actions of the other branches, remains unclear in some areas.

The checks and balances and court cases interpreting the Constitution's grant of government power play an important role in the development of the rule of law. They have helped ensure that no branch of the government rises above the law. Various laws and procedures also make it difficult for government officials to operate beyond the reach of the law.

LEGISLATIVE POWER

Article I of the U.S Constitution gives Congress a wide range of powers. The powers actually stated in the Constitution are known as Congress's enumerated powers. The Constitution gives Congress the authority to establish and maintain armed forces. It gives it the power to declare war. Congress also has the power to print money and collect taxes. It can propose new Constitutional amendments. It can admit new states to the Union. Congress can also set up federal courts.

The Constitution also gives Congress the power to "regulate commerce with foreign nations, and with the Indian tribes." This section of the Constitution is known as the Commerce Clause. Over the years, the Commerce

President Barack Obama delivers his State of the Union address to the U.S. Congress.

Clause has served as the source of much of Congress's legislative power. The Commerce Clause allows Congress to pass laws touching on a wide range of issues. The U.S. Supreme Court has ruled that Congress has a lot of discretion when deciding to regulate activities that affect interstate commerce. As long as a specific statute passed by Congress is reasonably related to achieving the goal of regulating foreign or interstate commerce, the legislation falls within the powers of Congress.

The Commerce Clause does not give Congress the power to enact any law it wants. Some laws have failed to satisfy the "reasonable relationship" standard. For example, in *Lopez v. United States* (1995), the Supreme Court ruled that Congress could not pass a law that prohibited people from carrying handguns into schools. The Court struck down the federal Gun Free School Zones Act of 1990. It held that the federal government has no authority under the Commerce Clause to regulate firearms in local schools. The Court ruled that the possession of guns at schools was not reasonably related to Congress's power to regulate interstate commerce. The issue of handguns in schools is a local one. The Court ruled that only state legislatures had the power to enact laws banning guns in its schools.

Article I also grants Congress the power to "provide for . . . the general welfare of the United States."

U.S. Supreme Court decisions have upheld the power of Congress under the General Welfare Clause to attach conditions when giving federal funds to states. For example, the Court upheld Congress's right to require states to have a maximum speed limit of 55 miles (89 kilometers) per hour in order to receive federal transportation funds. States could set higher speed limits, but Congress had the power to refuse to send them money. Likewise, in *South Dakota v. Dole* (1987), the Court upheld the National Minimum Drinking Age Act. It set twenty-one as the minimum age to consume alcoholic beverages. The Court ruled that Congress could withhold federal transportation funds from a state that had a drinking age lower than twenty-one years.

The Constitution gives Congress the power to "make all Laws which shall be necessary and proper for carrying into Execution the foregoing Powers, and all other Powers vested by this Constitution in the Government of the United States." In its landmark *McCulloch v. Maryland* (1819) decision, the Supreme Court ruled that the Necessary and Proper Clause grants Congress a wide range of powers that aren't spelled out in the Constitution. These powers are known as Congress's implied powers. Congress has exercised many implied powers. They have ranged from setting nationwide minimum-wage laws to establishing national parks.

Article I also lists several powers that Congress does not have. Congress cannot enact ex post facto laws. (In Latin, *ex post facto* means "after the fact.") This means that Congress cannot pass a law that makes an action or behavior that occurred before the law was enacted illegal. Congress also cannot grant a title of nobility to anyone. Several of the amendments to the Constitution prohibit Congress from making laws that infringe on free speech, freedom of religion, and many other individual liberties.

The Constitution also governs the relationship between Congress and the fifty states. Many activities and fields of law are considered state issues. These are areas in which, customarily or legally, only state

The U.S. Supreme Court building is in Washington, D.C. The Supreme Court, the nation's highest court, hears appeals from lower courts and tries specific types of cases.

legislatures can regulate. For example, state laws have traditionally governed most crimes. States also have the sole power to supply certain governmental services, such as education.

The Constitution gives the executive and judicial branches the authority to limit Congress's power. Article I requires presidential approval of every bill or other legislation passed by Congress. A president can refuse to sign a bill. This act is known as a veto. Congress can override a president's veto if a two-thirds majority of both the House of Representatives and the Senate vote to approve the vetoed bill. For example, in 2006 President George W. Bush vetoed a bill that made it easier for the federal government to provide money for embryonic stem cell research. The House and the Senate overrode Bush's veto. The Stem Cell Enhancement Act became law.

The Supreme Court has the power to declare any law passed by Congress unconstitutional. For example, in 1933 Congress passed the National Industrial Recovery Act (NIRA). This law allowed business groups to propose various safety codes for their industries. It also gave the president authority to give these codes legal effect. Federal officials charged the officers of a poultry company with violating an NIRA code by selling sick chickens. In *A.L.A. Schecter Poultry Corp. v. United States* (1935), the U.S. Supreme Court held that NIRA was unconstitutional. It ruled that

Congress could not delegate its legislative powers over certain local issues. In this case, the poultry company bought and sold chickens in only one state. The Court ruled that the Constitution does not allow the federal government to exercise "uncontrolled police power in every state of the Union, superseding all local control or regulation of the affairs or concerns of the states." With this decision, the Court affirmed that the Constitution sets limits on the legislative powers of Congress.

Voters also have the ability to affect the power of Congress. They can influence their representatives to vote in certain ways. They can elect new representatives to repeal unpopular federal laws.

EXECUTIVE POWER

The Constitution assigns only a few powers for the executive branch. Article II gives executive powers to the president. The executive branch is responsible for enforcing the laws passed by Congress. The president also directs the work of various departments, such as the Department of Defense. He oversees federal agencies, such as the Federal Communications Commission.

The Constitution names the president as the commander-in-chief of the nation's armed forces. The president appoints top military commanders. He has the authority to order federal troops into

action to deal with distur-
bances in the United States
and in foreign countries.
The Constitution also
places the president in
charge of the nation's foreign policy. The executive
branch oversees diplomatic
relations with other
nations. It negotiates treaties with other countries.
The president has the
authority to appoint ambas-
sadors and other diplomats.

Although the Constitution
gives Congress all legislative
powers, the president can use
his influence to get laws
passed. He may pressure or
persuade members of
Congress to pass a bill. The
Constitution gives the president the power to call
Congress into a special session
to pass important legislation.
For example, in 2005
President Bush called a special
session of Congress to pass a

President Barack Obama addresses a joint session of Congress. Obama sought to convince members to vote for a jobs bill supported by his administration.

disaster aid bill to help the victims of Hurricane Katrina. If the president calls a special session, Congress must meet. The Constitution, however, does not require it to pass any legislation during the session.

The legislative and judicial branches can limit the power of the executive branch. The ability of these two branches to restrain the actions of the executive branch is vitally important. The executive branch has the power to enforce law. Its officials are in the best position to ignore the principles of the rule of law. The Senate must approve all treaties negotiated by the executive branch. Only Congress has the power to declare war. Under federal law, Congress must issue an official declaration of war if the president sends troops into an international conflict for more than ninety days. Congress can also control a president's military powers by withholding funding from the military. The Senate must also approve a president's appointments for cabinet posts and federal judges, including Supreme Court justices. The Supreme Court may declare actions and decisions of the president and other executive branch officials unconstitutional.

Impeachment is the ultimate control on the power of the president. The Constitution provides a method for removing a president from office if he breaks the law. The House of Representatives may vote to bring impeachment charges for "treason, bribery or other high crimes, and misdemeanors." Treason is an act

OATHS OF OFFICE

All officers of the federal government pledge to uphold the Constitution. The congressional oath reads:

> I do solemnly swear (or affirm) that I will support and defend the Constitution of the United States against all enemies, foreign and domestic; that I will bear true faith and allegiance to the same; that I take this obligation freely, without any mental reservation or purpose of evasion; and that I will well and faithfully discharge the duties of the office on which I am about to enter: So help me God.

By pledging to preserve the Constitution, members of Congress, presidents, judges, and other government officials affirm that they are subject to the rule of law.

that betrays one's own country. The exact definition of "high crimes" and "misdemeanors" is unclear.

If the House of Representatives votes to impeach a president, then the Senate conducts a trial. The chief justice of the Supreme Court presides over the trial. If a two-thirds majority of the Senate votes for a conviction, the president is removed from office. The House has voted to impeach two presidents. In Bill Clinton's trial, the Senate voted 55–45 to acquit, or find not guilty, on one charge and 50–50 on another charge. In Andrew Johnson's case, the Senate voted 35–19 in

Members of President Bill Clinton's legal team enter the chambers of the U.S. Senate. The lawyers argued on behalf of Clinton during his impeachment trial conducted by the Senate.

favor of guilty. That was one vote short of the required two-thirds majority to remove Johnson from office.

JUDICIAL POWER

The Constitution limits the power of the federal judiciary. Article III specifies what types of "cases and controversies" federal courts can hear. It gives federal courts jurisdiction, or the power to hear a case, over two categories of cases. Federal courts have jurisdiction over all cases that involve a constitutional issue, a federal law, or a treaty. This category includes lawsuits between states, cases involving high-ranking U.S. government officials, and foreign diplomats. It includes cases involving a federal crime, bankruptcy, or a patent, trademark, or copyright.

Federal courts also have jurisdiction over certain civil lawsuits in which the two opposing parties are residents of different states. The amount of money involved in the lawsuit must be more than $75,000 for a federal court to hear the case.

A state court may interpret federal laws and the Constitution if they are related to its case. However, the Supreme Court has the authority to review any state court's interpretation of federal or constitutional law. The Supreme Court may overturn a state court's verdict if it is based on a federal or constitutional issue.

The Supreme Court has the power to invalidate any law enacted by Congress that conflicts with the

Constitution. The Court claimed this power in the landmark case of *Marbury v. Madison* (1803). The issue in *Marbury* centered on whether federal officials who violated the law must submit to a judicial order. The Court ruled that the judicial branch could enforce the law on all citizens, including government officials. In his opinion, Chief Justice John Marshall asserted that the Constitution is the supreme law of the country. He wrote that the Constitution is "a superior paramount law, unchangeable by ordinary means." If a law enacted by Congress conflicts with the Constitution, then courts have a duty to invalidate it. Otherwise, Marshall argued, Congress could change the Constitution by merely passing a law.

The U.S. legal system is based on the principle that legal precedents establish the law. Courts generally adopt the rulings of other courts that have previously decided the same or similar issue. In general, lower courts must follow the precedents established by higher courts. The Supreme Court, however, is not bound by the rulings of lower courts. The Supreme Court sometimes overrules its own precedent by making a different ruling on the same issue. This usually occurs when conditions in society have changed. For example, in *Brown v. Board of Education* (1954), the Supreme Court ruled that a state law requiring separate public schools for black and white students was unconstitutional. The Court's decision invalidated the

The nine justices of the U.S. Supreme Court pose for a photograph in October 2010. The Supreme Court has the power to strike down laws that it deems violate the U.S. Constitution.

existing separate-but-equal doctrine, which an earlier Supreme Court had established as constitutional in *Plessy v. Ferguson* (1896).

The executive and legislative branches have the ability to limit the power of the judiciary. The president and the Senate control which judges are appointed as federal judges, including Supreme Court justices. The Constitution gives the president authority to nominate a person for a federal judgeship. The Senate must approve the appointment of all federal judges.

The Senate Judiciary Committee usually holds a confirmation hearing to ask the nominee questions. The committee then writes a report for the full Senate. The report either supports or opposes the appointment. The full Senate then votes to confirm or reject the nomination. If the Senate confirms the nomination, the new federal judge has a lifetime appointment. Like a president, a federal judge may be removed from office through the impeachment process. Federal judges are rarely impeached. In 2010, Judge Thomas Porteous became only the eighth federal judge to be removed from office.

Congress also has a means to limit the power of the judiciary branch. In *Chisholm v. Georgia* (1793), the Supreme Court ruled that federal courts had jurisdiction over a lawsuit filed against the State of Georgia by a citizen of South Carolina. State leaders were unhappy with the Court's decision. The following year, Congress passed a resolution proposing the Eleventh Amendment. It would invalidate the Court's decision in *Chisholm*. The states ratified the amendment in 1795. The Eleventh Amendment provides that the federal judiciary does not have jurisdiction over cases in which a state is sued by a citizen of another state or a citizen of another country.

I ssues and controversies involving the rule of law have arisen throughout the history of the United States. The rule of law places restrictions on the powers of the three branches of government. All three branches have used their authority under the Constitution to control another branch's use of governmental power.

The rule of law also limits the discretion of government officials who enforce laws and make administrative decisions. The Constitution and federal law do not spell out exactly how much discretion every government official has. Laws, court cases, and government rules have established a framework to guide government officials in carrying out their legal duties. But in administering the government and enforcing laws, government officials often make decisions or take actions that may be beyond their legal authority. The ability of government officials to make decisions outside the law poses a constant threat to the rule of law.

First Amendment Rights

The First Amendment to the Constitution includes guarantees of freedom of speech and

PROTECTION OF INDIVIDUAL RIGHTS

One of the primary benefits of the rule of law is that it helps guarantee individual rights. In the United States, citizens sometimes have to file lawsuits to protect their rights. Legislatures, often following the desires of the majority or of special interest groups, have passed laws that encroached on individual rights.

Presidents, governors, and other government officials have enforced laws unfairly or arbitrarily. Federal and state courts have struck down laws when they violated rights guaranteed in the U.S. Constitution or state constitutions. These cases have helped define the limits of government power and the supremacy of the rule of law. When a government official takes away, denies, or infringes on the rights of individuals, the rule of law is harmed.

freedom of the press. It also prohibits Congress from passing laws that restrict the rights of citizens to assemble or to petition the government for a redress of grievances. The founders of the nation who wrote and approved the Bill of Rights had firsthand knowledge of the importance of the freedom of speech and the freedom of the press. They had been denied both rights by British colonial officials. The founders wanted to guarantee that future generations would have the right to speak freely, even to disagree openly with government policies. The right to challenge government decisions without worrying about being arrested or punished is a cornerstone of political freedom.

Although the First Amendment seems to make the freedom of speech and of the press absolute, courts have placed limits on them. The Supreme Court has approved laws that require a permit to hold political rallies and other public assemblies. However, officials cannot use a permit system to restrict or deny free speech or assembly.

Courts have also invalidated laws that restrict free speech. In *Brandenburg v. Ohio* (1968), the Supreme Court considered the case of a Ku Klux Klan leader who had been convicted of advocating violence in a speech. The Court ruled that the state statute prohibiting any public speech that advocates various criminal, violent, or other illegal activities to bring about political change was invalid. It violated the First Amendment right to free speech. The Court adopted a two-part test for free speech. The government can prohibit speech if it is "directed at inciting or producing imminent lawless action" and is also "likely to incite or produce such action."

In *Texas v. Johnson* (1989), the Supreme Court heard the case of Gregory Lee Johnson. He had been convicted under a state law that prohibited desecrating the U.S. flag. In a 5–4 decision, the Court ruled that Johnson's act of burning a U.S. flag was protected

Occupy Wall Street protesters march in New York City. The First Amendment protects the right of citizens to demonstrate peacefully.

under the First Amendment. The Court reasoned that flag burning is a type of conduct that expresses a political message. In his majority opinion, Justice William Brennan wrote, "If there is a bedrock principle underlying the First Amendment, it is that the Government may not prohibit the expression of an idea simply because society finds the idea itself offensive or disagreeable."

Rule of law controversies often arise in legal cases involving freedom of the press. In 1971, the *New York Times* published secret government documents that discussed government decisions involving the ongoing Vietnam War. Richard Nixon's administration asked a federal court to issue an order to prevent the newspaper from publishing the documents. It argued that publication

Police officers in Dallas, Texas, arrest Gregory Johnson after he protested by burning a U.S. flag. Five years later, the U.S. Supreme Court ruled that the Texas statute outlawing the burning of a U.S. flag violated the First Amendment.

would harm national security interests. In *United States v. New York Times*, the Supreme Court held that the government could not stop the publication of the documents. In upholding the newspaper's First Amendment rights, Justice Hugo Black wrote, "Only a free and unrestrained press can effectively expose deception in government."

Religious Freedoms

The First Amendment also guarantees freedom of religion. It separates freedom of religion into two parts. The Free Exercise Clause prohibits the government from interfering with a person's practice of religion in most cases. The Establishment Clause prevents the government from establishing a religion. Government actions and decisions cannot prefer one religion over another. They also cannot aid one religion or all religions.

When people talk about the separation of church and state, they are talking about the Establishment Clause.

An ongoing controversy involving First Amendment religious rights is prayer in public schools. In *Engel v. Vitale* (1961), the Supreme Court ruled that a New York regulation allowing public schools to hold a voluntary, nondenominational prayer recitation at the start of each school day violated the First Amendment's Establishment Clause. The Court ruled that by providing the prayer, the state was officially approving religion.

States later passed laws requiring a moment of silent reflection before the start of the school day. For example, Virginia enacted a law that required students to begin the day with a minute of silence. Students could pray, meditate, or engage in any silent activity. A federal court upheld the law. It noted that the law allowed any type of silent reflection, not just prayer. The U.S. Supreme Court declined to hear the case on appeal.

Search and Seizure

The Fourth Amendment guarantees citizens the right "to be secure in their persons, houses, papers, and effects, against unreasonable searches and seizures." In most cases, a law enforcement officer may search or seize a person or his or her property only under certain circumstances. The officer must have either a search warrant or an arrest warrant issued by a judge or magistrate. If the officer does not have a warrant, he or she must have probable cause to believe that the person has committed a crime.

Courts have made several major exceptions to the general rule regarding searches and seizures. If a police officer stops a driver for a traffic violation, the officer can seize any evidence of a crime that is in plain sight. For example, if an officer spots illegal drugs in the car, he or she may seize the drugs as evidence and arrest the driver or passengers.

Police officers in Shreveport, Louisiana, search an apartment for drugs. The tenant had given the officers permission to search the home.

In *Terry v. Ohio* (1967), the Supreme Court established another exception. It upheld the defendant's conviction for carrying a concealed weapon. A police officer noticed John W. Terry and two other men acting strangely. He believed that they were preparing to commit a robbery. The officer stopped the men and frisked them. He found a weapon on Terry and arrested him. The Court ruled that police officers may stop a person and search for weapons if they believe that the person is armed and presents a threat to the officer or to the public. The Court observed that the officer must have a reasonable suspicion, not merely a hunch, that the person is armed. If the officer finds an illegal weapon or evidence of another crime, he can seize the evidence without a warrant.

The Right to a Fair Trial

The rule of law requires that judicial proceedings follow established procedures and be conducted fairly. Supreme Court decisions have defined the rights of people accused and charged with crimes. In *Gideon v. Wainright* (1963), the Court ruled that the Sixth Amendment's guarantee of counsel was a fundamental right that guaranteed a fair trial. If a defendant cannot afford an attorney, a court will appoint one at public expense. *Gideon* applied only to felony cases. Later court decisions expanded the right to free counsel to misdemeanors and other charges in which the defendant faces the possibility of jail time. Defendants do not have the right of free counsel for traffic violations or other charges that are punishable only by fines. The right to court-appointed counsel also applies to juvenile proceedings.

In *Miranda v. Arizona* (1965), the Court expanded the right to counsel beyond courtroom representation. During a police interrogation, Ernesto Miranda confessed to committing a rape. He was then convicted and sentenced to a prison term. Miranda appealed his conviction, arguing that the police interrogators did not notify him of his Sixth Amendment right to counsel and his Fifth Amendment right not to incriminate himself. The Court ruled that prosecutors may not use statements made by suspects before police inform them of their right to counsel and their right to remain silent. It held that government prosecutors may use statements made by a person accused of a crime as evidence only if the person "voluntarily, knowingly, and intelligently" waived his or her right to remain silent. Prosecutors, law enforcement officials, and many citizens criticized the Court's decision. They argued that fewer criminals would confess to crime, making it more difficult for prosecutors to win convictions. Later Supreme Court cases narrowed the *Miranda* decision, creating many exceptions to the general rule.

In 1967, Ernesto Miranda appeared in an Arizona court after the U.S. Supreme Court overturned his conviction. Since *Miranda v. Arizona*, law enforcement officers have been required to inform arrestees of their right to remain silent and their right to legal counsel.

Minority Rights

An important aspect of the rule of law is that it protects the rights of a society's minorities. Throughout the history of the United States, African Americans and other minorities have suffered the economic and personal costs of discrimination. Racial discrimination occurs when an individual receives unequal treatment because of his or her actual or assumed race.

When the United States was founded, slavery was legal in most states. The ratification of the Fourteenth Amendment in 1865 ended it. The amendment gave African Americans equal rights with all other citizens—on paper. Some states, particularly in the South, passed various laws that separated white and black citizens. In *Plessy v. Ferguson* (1896), the Supreme Court upheld a Louisiana law that required black and white railroad passengers to sit in separate cars. The Court ruled that separate facilities for blacks and whites did not violate the Fourteenth Amendment's guarantee of equal protection under the law as long as the facilities were equal. The Court's separate-but-equal doctrine provided the foundation for legal segregation. In states that legalized segregation, the schools and other facilities for black citizens were rarely equal to those of white citizens.

Nearly sixty years later, the Supreme Court unanimously overturned the separate-but-equal doctrine. In *Brown v. Board of Education* (1954), the Court invalidated state laws that segregated public school students based solely on race. It ruled that segregation laws violated the equal protection clause of the Fourteenth Amendment. Chief Justice Earl Warren wrote that the separate-but-equal doctrine "has no place" in public education. He also noted, "Separate educational facilities are inherently unequal."

Brown was the first of many Supreme Court decisions that ended legal racial segregation in all areas of society. In *Heart of Atlanta Motel v. United States* (1964), the Court upheld a section of the Civil Rights Act that outlawed racial discrimination by restaurants, hotels, and other places of public accommodation. It confirmed the conviction of the Heart of Atlanta Motel for violating the act by refusing to accept African Americans as customers. In *Loving v. Virginia* (1966), the Court ruled that the state's law forbidding interracial marriages violated the equal protection clause.

To achieve a diverse student body that includes racial minorities, some law schools, medical schools, and colleges began giving special consideration to minority students applying for admission.

White students filed lawsuits claiming affirmative action programs violated the Fourteenth Amendment's equal protection clause. In *Regents of the University of California v. Bakke* (1977), the Court considered whether an affirmative action program violated the equal protection clause or the Civil Rights Act of 1964. The University of California Medical School at Davis twice rejected Allan Bakke's application for admission. The school had an admissions policy that reserved sixteen spots for minorities in each entering class of one hundred students. Bakke's qualifications exceeded those of many of the minority students the school admitted. In a complicated decision, four justices ruled that the schools admission policy violated the Civil Rights Act. One justice ruled that it violated the equal protection clause. By a 5–4 majority, the Court ordered the school to admit Bakke because its use of racial quotas was illegal. However, five of the justices agreed that schools can use race as one of the factors in their admissions policies.

In *Grutter v. Bollinger* (2002), the Supreme Court held that the University of Michigan Law School's admission policies did not violate the equal protection clause. The Court noted that the school's admission policy included race as only one factor in its efforts to achieve a diverse student population.

The school's admissions procedure considered a wide range of factors. Because race was not a major factor in the school's admissions decisions, its affirmative action policy produced little harm to white applicants.

CORRUPTION IN GOVERNMENT

One of the goals of the rule of law is to ensure that government officials follow laws and established procedures when making official decisions. Government officials must carry out their duties fairly. They must avoid taking actions based on their personal preferences.

Various forms of government corruption, such as taking bribes or favoring some groups over others, harm taxpayers. When

On August 9, 1974, President Richard Nixon announced his resignation. Public and political pressure for Nixon to resign arose when the Watergate scandal engulfed his administration and Congress appeared ready to impeach him.

government officials use their offices for personal or financial gain, it undermines the integrity of the government. For example, a company may offer an Environmental Protection Agency official money or a promise of a future job if he overlooks a violation of environment laws. If the official accepts the company's bribe and allows the company to break the law, his actions undermine the public interest.

Throughout the history of the United States, government officials have been prosecuted or forced to resign for engaging in public corruption. Public corruption is a breach of trust by federal, state, or local officials. It often occurs with the assistance of private individuals or groups. In the nineteenth century, nearly a dozen corruption scandals plagued the administration of President Ulysses Grant. The cover-up of a break-in ordered by his reelection committee forced President Richard Nixon to resign in 1974. In 2005, Justice Department investigators uncovered a corruption scandal involving lobbyist Jack Abramoff. Its investigation resulted in the convictions of twenty-one people, including congressional aides, government officials, and one former member of Congress. Former representative Robert Ney was convicted of trading political favors for gifts and campaign donations coordinated by Abramoff.

Over the past few decades, public-interest groups that monitor the government have criticized the growing practice of government workers using their public service to advance their careers. Many public servants have used their government jobs as a stepping-stone to working in the private sector. A revolving door between government jobs and private enterprise jobs has created a situation in which the public interest has been damaged. When regulators become too cozy with the regulated, the government may not enforce laws fairly or at all.

THE FUTURE OF THE RULE OF LAW

In the twenty-first century, the integrity of the rule of law in the United States has been challenged in many ways. The nation's massive campaign to fight against terrorism has resulted in new laws and executive branch decisions that conflict with the rule of law. A financial crisis and long-lasting economic slump exposed the weak government regulation of financial and banking industries. Many citizens, particularly young people, began to worry about the growing inequality between the nation's rich and the poor. They wondered whether the level economic playing field that their parents and grandparents benefited from still existed.

While questions persisted about the weakening of the rule of law in the United States, the United Nations and other agencies sought to expand the rule of law worldwide. These organizations work with the governments in developing countries to install laws and policies that strengthen the rule of law. The hope is that the rule of law will help these countries form stronger governments, more robust economies, and fairer societies.

THE WAR ON TERRORISM

In response to the September 11, 2001, terrorist attacks, Congress passed legislation that authorized the president to "use all necessary and appropriate force against those nations, organizations, or persons he determines planned, authorized, committed, or aided" the attacks. In October 2001, the United States, along with several allies, invaded Afghanistan. Osama bin Laden and other Al Qaeda leaders used

A guard patrols the fence at the U.S. military prison at Guantánamo Bay, Cuba. The issue of trying terrorism suspects detained by the military has challenged Congress, federal courts, and the executive branch.

the country as its base. The U.S. military detained hundreds of people suspected of being involved in the September 11 attacks. These detainees were transported to the U.S. naval base at Guantánamo Bay in Cuba.

Military Commissions

U.S. government officials faced the issue of how to determine the guilt of the suspected terrorists in their custody. The Bush administration sought swift justice. It wanted to avoid having the detainees tried in federal, state, or military courts. These courts had rules and procedures that made it more difficult to get a guilty verdict. Instead of treating the detainees as criminals or prisoners of war, the administration declared that they were illegal enemy combatants. The Defense Department would try the terror suspects in special military commissions.

The military commissions would operate outside the U.S. judiciary. Several countries and the United Nations Commission on Human Rights declared that the United States was violating due process and internationally accepted rules for the treatment of detainees. In 2011, President Barack Obama also signed an executive order that continued the Bush administration policy of detaining terror suspects without a trial.

In 2005, the U.S. Supreme Court agreed to hear a case involving Guantánamo detainees. U.S. forces had taken custody of Salim Hamdan in 2001. He had worked as a driver for Bin Laden. In 2004, the U.S. government charged Hamdan with conspiracy to commit offenses that can be tried by a military commission. Along with other Guantánamo detainees, he filed a petition in federal court. Hamdan's lawyers

A military court convicted Salim Hamdan on terrorism charges in 2005, but the U.S. Supreme Court overturned the conviction. In 2008, a special military commission convicted Hamdan of providing material support to Al Qaeda.

argued that his upcoming trial before a military commission was illegal. The federal district court ruled in his favor. The U.S. Court of Appeals, however, reversed the decision.

In *Hamdan v. Rumsfeld* (2005), the Supreme Court ruled that neither federal law nor the constitutional powers of the president authorized the type of military commissions the Defense Department would be using. Congress, however, soon passed the Detainee Treatment Act of 2005. This law prevented federal courts from hearing cases filed by detainees at Guantánamo Bay. Hamdan was later charged with providing material support to Al Qaeda. A military commission sentenced him to five years in prison. He was later transferred to his home country of Yemen. He served the rest of his prison term. Hamdan was released from a Yemeni jail in 2009.

National Security

In conducting the fight against terrorism, the Bush administration adopted other controversial policies. Its lawyers argued that the president had broad powers to ignore existing legal boundaries if the security of the nation required it. These policies appeared to conflict with the rule of law. The administration ignored federal laws and international standards that prohibit secret detentions and torture. It also authorized the National Security Agency to listen to

TORTURE MEMOS

In the wake of the 2001 terrorist attacks, the Bush administration composed several controversial legal memos that supported the administration's conduct of the war on terror. The Office of Legal Counsel, which is part of the Justice Department, issued memos that provided legal rationales for using various interrogation techniques to get information from suspected terrorists in custody. One memo provided complex definitions of methods that critics argued were torture. These definitions appeared to critics to allow government and military interrogators to avoid being charged with torture.

Both U.S. federal law and the Geneva Conventions forbid the use of torture. The Geneva Conventions are treaties that govern the treatment of prisoners of war. When the memos were released to the public in 2009, critics argued that they were written to give legal immunity to government officials who committed acts that were illegal. Critics also noted that the government lawyers who wrote the memos did not fulfill their duties to provide unbiased advice on the legality of various interrogation techniques.

telephone calls and read e-mails that Americans send abroad without obtaining a warrant. Federal law requires government officials to get a warrant to eavesdrop on U.S. citizens. None of the government officials who may have broken this law were investigated or charged with a crime.

Drone Assassinations

In September 2011, a drone aircraft operated by the U.S. Central Intelligence Agency fired a missile at a vehicle traveling along a roadway in Yemen. The missile struck the vehicle, killing two members of Al Qaeda, Anwar al-Awlaki and Samir Khan. Both men were American citizens. President Obama had ordered the killing, calling Awlaki "the leader of the external operations for Al Qaeda in the Arabian Peninsula." Awlaki was also accused of encouraging Muslims to fight against the United States in his speeches and writings. Khan worked as an editor of *Inspire*, Al Qaeda's English-language online magazine. Government lawyers argued that the process

An MQ-9 Reaper drone flies over Nevada during a 2008 training mission. The use of unmanned aircraft to kill suspected terrorists, including U.S. citizens, by the Bush and Obama administrations ignited controversy over the scope of executive branch powers.

the executive branch used to approve these targeted killings satisfied the requirements of due process.

Civil rights activists condemned the killings of Awlaki and Khan. They pointed out that the Fifth Amendment prohibits the government from depriving U.S. citizens of life without due process of law. They argued that the executive branch could not decide what constituted due process. They also noted that Awlaki and Khan were targeted for their radical Islamic sermons and articles. Those rights may be protected by the First Amendment. Despite the uproar, a U.S. drone attack killed Awlaki's sixteen-year-old son, Abdulrahman, and eight other people in October 2010. The teenager was also a U.S. citizen. Government officials claimed that he was a terrorist operative.

PRESIDENTIAL SIGNING STATEMENTS

A president issues a written signing statement when he signs a bill into law. James Monroe is believed to be the first president to publish a signing statement. George W. Bush caused controversy with some of his signing statements. These signing statements asserted that the Bush administration would not enforce a law that conflicted with the powers granted to the president by the Constitution. Critics noted that the use of this type of signing statements allows a president to avoid vetoing a bill he does not like. A veto could have political consequences. These signing statements also prevented Congress from overriding his veto.

In July 2006, a special committee of the American Bar Association published a report that concluded that some of Bush's signing statements undermined "the rule of law and our constitutional systems of separation of powers." The committee noted that the Constitution gives a president two options. He must either veto the legislation or sign it and execute the laws faithfully. If a president signs a law but does not execute it faithfully, it weakens the rule of law.

SPREADING THE RULE OF LAW

The United Nations and other international agencies work to develop the rule of law worldwide. The UN conducts programs that support the development of the rule of law in more than one hundred countries around the world. It helps nations draft constitutions and laws that hold government officials accountable. The UN also helps countries build strong legal systems and train lawyers, judges, and government officials.

The UN General Assembly and UN Security Council encourage the development of international law standards. Its Peacebuilding Commission and Human Rights Council work to strengthen individual

The United Nations sponsors programs that support and strengthen the rule of law in countries around the world.

rights worldwide. The International Court of Justice, the UN's judiciary, conducts trials to uphold international law and protect human rights.

PRESERVING THE RULE OF LAW

Nations adopt the rule of law to avoid the arbitrary or discretionary rule of government authorities. Under the rule of law, government officials must faithfully enforce laws and follow established procedures. In contrast, under the rule of authority, government officials have the power to make new laws as they wish. They can enforce laws any way they want or ignore them altogether.

The rule of law remains vulnerable in the United States and other countries. It is effective only when government institutions and citizens hold government officials accountable for their actions. During times of war or civil unrest, government officials stress national security as the reason to weaken or deny individual rights. The rule of law does not prevent legislators from enacting laws that are unfair to individuals, minorities, or other groups. It does not prevent executive branch officials from enforcing laws arbitrarily. The U.S. Constitution provides the means to preserve the rule of law. Citizens and public servants must remain vigilant to ensure that no person, government official, or group rises above the law.

PREAMBLE TO THE CONSTITUTION

We the People of the United States, in order to form a more perfect Union, establish Justice, insure domestic Tranquility, provide for the common defense, promote the general Welfare, and secure the Blessings of Liberty to ourselves and our Posterity, do ordain and establish this Constitution for the United States of America.

On September 25, 1789, Congress transmitted to the state legislatures twelve proposed amendments, two of which, having to do with congressional representation and congressional pay, were not adopted. The remaining ten amendments became the Bill of Rights.

THE BILL OF RIGHTS

Amendment I

Congress shall make no law respecting an establishment of religion, or prohibiting the free exercise thereof; or abridging the freedom of speech, or of the press; or the right of the people peaceably to assemble, and to petition the Government for a redress of grievances.

Amendment II

A well regulated Militia, being necessary to the security of a free State, the right of the people to keep and bear Arms, shall not be infringed.

Amendment III

No Soldier shall, in time of peace be quartered in any house, without the consent of the Owner, nor in time of war, but in a manner to be prescribed by law.

Amendment IV

The right of the people to be secure in their persons, houses, papers, and effects, against unreasonable searches and seizures, shall not be violated, and no Warrants shall issue, but upon probable cause, supported by Oath or affirmation, and particularly describing the place to be searched, and the persons or things to be seized.

Amendment V

No person shall be held to answer for a capital, or otherwise infamous crime, unless on a presentment or indictment of a Grand Jury, except in cases arising in the land or naval forces, or in the Militia, when in actual service in time of War or public danger; nor shall any person be subject for the same offence to be twice put in jeopardy of life or limb; nor shall be compelled in any criminal case to be a witness against himself, nor be deprived of life, liberty, or property, without due process of law; nor shall private property be taken for public use, without just compensation.

Amendment VI

In all criminal prosecutions, the accused shall enjoy the right to a speedy and public trial, by an impartial jury of the State and district wherein the crime shall have been committed, which district shall have been previously ascertained by law, and to be informed of the nature and cause of the accusation; to be confronted with the witnesses against him; to have compulsory process for obtaining witnesses in his favor, and to have the Assistance of Counsel for his defense.

Amendment VII

In Suits at common law, where the value in controversy shall exceed twenty dollars, the right of trial by jury shall be preserved, and no fact tried by a jury, shall be otherwise reexamined in any Court of the United States, than according to the rules of the common law.

Amendment VIII

Excessive bail shall not be required, nor excessive fines imposed, nor cruel and unusual punishments inflicted.

Amendment IX

The enumeration in the Constitution, of certain rights, shall not be construed to deny or disparage others retained by the people.

Amendment X

The powers not delegated to the United States by the Constitution, nor prohibited by it to the States, are reserved to the States respectively, or to the people.

affirmative action Policies that improve the educational or employment opportunities for members of minority groups.

amendment A change to the U.S. Constitution.

arbitrary Acting in any manner one sees fit; something not based on sound reasons.

boycott To join with others in refusing to buy items from a person, business, or nation.

checks and balances A political and legal structure that allows each branch of a government to limit the power of other branches.

colony A territory claimed by the country that settles it.

constitution A document that states the basic principles used to govern a state or country.

corruption Behavior that violates the law or tries to interfere with the enforcement of laws.

discretion The power to make a decision within certain boundaries.

due process The procedures in the judicial system that respect the rights of individuals.

enumerated power A power of Congress that is specifically mentioned in the Constitution.

implied power A power of Congress that the framers intended to give but did not express in the Constitution.

infringe To go beyond the legal limits.

jurisdiction A court's power and right to hear a case.

justice Right treatment or action.

popular sovereignty The theory that a government is created by citizens and is subject to their desires.

precedent A decision, such as a court case, that serves as an example to be followed in the future.

repeal To cancel an existing law, sometimes by replacing it with a new law.

separation of powers The balance of authority between the three branches of the U.S. government.

veto To refuse to sign a law passed by a legislature; means "I forbid" in Latin.

The Canadian Justice Review Board

Box 4853 Station E

Ottawa, ON K1S 5J1

Canada

Web site: http://www.canadianjusticereviewboard.ca

The Canadian Justice Review Board provides information about the Constitution of Canada, Canadian laws, and the rule of law in Canada.

The National Archives

700 Pennsylvania Avenue NW

Washington, DC 20408

(866) 272-6272

Web site: http://www.archives.gov

The National Archives provides the texts of the Declaration of Independence, the Constitution, and the Bill of Rights.

OMB Watch

1742 Connecticut Avenue NW

Washington, DC 20009

(202) 234-8494

Web site: http://www.ombwatch.org

OMB Watch is a nonprofit organization that researches and publicizes the decisions and actions of the White House Office of Management and Budget (OMB). The OMB is an executive branch agency that helps the president budget and implement the enforcement of federal laws.

The United Nations

1 United Nations Plaza

New York, NY 10017
(212) 963-1234
Web site: http://www.unrol.org
The United Nations provides information on efforts to develop the
rule of law in countries around the world.

U.S. House of Representatives
Washington, DC 20515
(202) 224-3121
Web site: http://www.house.gov
The House of Representatives provides information on how
Congress and the other two branches of the government operate.

The White House
1600 Pennsylvania Avenue NW
Washington, DC 20500
(202) 456-1414
Web site: http://www.whitehouse.gov
The White House provides information on the executive branch
and on how the U.S. government works.

WEB SITES

Due to the changing nature of Internet links, Rosen
Publishing has developed an online list of Web sites
related to the subject of this book. This site is updated
regularly. Please use this link to access the list:

http://www.rosenlinks.com/PFCD/Law

Brezina, Corona. *The Fifth Amendment*. New York,
NY: Rosen Publishing, 2011.

Brezina, Corona. *The Judicial Branch of the
Federal Government*. New York, NY: Rosen
Publishing, 2010.

Brezina, Corona. *The Legislative Branch of the
Federal Government*. New York, NY: Rosen
Publishing, 2010.

Friedman, Lauri S. *National Security*. Minneapolis,
MN: Lerner, 2010.

Friedman, Mark. *America's Struggle with Terrorism*.
New York, NY: Children's Press, 2012.

Hall, Kermit L., and James W. Ely, eds. *The Oxford
Guide to United States Supreme Court
Decisions*. New York, NY: Oxford University
Press, 2009.

Jones, Molly. *The First Amendment*. New York, NY:
Rosen Publishing, 2011.

Kowalski, Kathiann M. *Checks and Balances: A
Look at the Powers of Government*.
Minneapolis, MN: Lerner, 2012.

Kozlowski, Darrell J. *Federalism*. New York, NY:
Chelsea House, 2010.

Krensky, Stephen. *The Constitution*. New York, NY:
Marshall Cavendish, 2012.

Leavitt, Amie Jane. *The Bill of Rights*. Hockessin,
DE: Mitchell Lane, 2012.

Marston, Daniel. *The American Revolutionary War.* New York, NY: Rosen Publishing, 2011.

Miller, Mara. *Remembering September 11, 2001.* Berkeley Heights, NJ: Enslow, 2010.

Murphy, John. *The Impeachment Process.* New York, NY: Chelsea House, 2007.

Orr, Tamra. *The Story of the Constitution.* Hockessin, DE: Mitchell Lane, 2012.

Swain, Gwenyth. *Documents of Freedom.* Minneapolis, MN: Lerner, 2012.

American Civil Liberties Union. "Accountability for
Torture: The Bush Admin's Secret OLC Memos."
Retrieved August 20, 2012 (https://www.aclu
.org/accountability/olc.html).

Bardes, Barbara A., et al. *American Government and
Politics Today.* Boston, MA: Wadsworth, 2010.

Carothers, Thomas. "Democracy Policy Under
Obama." Carnegie Endowment for International
Peace. Retrieved August 21, 2012 (http://carnegie
endowment.org/2012/01/11/democracy-policy-
under-obama-revitalization-or-retreat).

Council of Europe. "Administrative Discretion and
the Rule of Law." Retrieved August 20, 2012
(http://www.venice.coe.int/docs/2010/CDL-
UDT(2010)022-e.asp).

Epstein, Richard A. *Design for Liberty: Private Property,
Public Administration, and the Rule of Law.*
Cambridge, MA: Harvard University Press, 2011.

Farnsworth, E. Allan. *An Introduction to the Legal
System of the United States.* New York, NY:
Oxford University Press, 2010.

FBI.gov. "Public Corruption: It's Our Top Priority
Among Criminal Investigations—and for Good
Reason." Retrieved August 20, 2012 (http://
www.fbi.gov/about-us/investigate/corruption).

Greenwald, Glenn. *With Liberty and Justice for
Some: How the Law Is Used to Destroy*

Equality and Protect the Powerful. New York,
NY: Metropolitan, 2011.

Holtzman, Elizabeth. *Cheating Justice.* Boston, MA:
Beacon Press, 2012.

Horton, Scott. "State of Exception: Bush's War on the
Rule of Law." *Harper's,* July 2007. Retrieved August
21, 2012 (http://harpers.org/archive/2007/07/
0081595).

Lansford, Tom, et al. *America's War on Terror.*
Burlington, VT: Ashgate, 2009.

Library of Congress. "Rule of Law Handbook."
Retrieved August 21, 2012 (http://www.loc.gov/rr/
frd/Military_Law/pdf/rule-of-law_2011.pdf).

Mahler, Jonathan. *The Challenge: Hamdan v. Rumsfeld
and the Fight over Presidential Power.* New York,
NY: Farrar, Straus and Giroux, 2008.

Pyle, Christopher H. *Getting Away with Torture.*
Washington, DC: Potomac, 2009.

Sanger, David E. *Confront and Conceal: Obama's Secret
Wars and Surprising Use of American Power.* New
York, NY: Crown, 2012.

Sarat, Austin, and Nasser Hussain, eds. *When
Governments Break the Law.* New York, NY: New
York University Press, 2010.

Schoenfeld, Gabriel. *Necessary Secrets: National
Security, the Media, and the Rule of Law.* New York,
NY: Norton, 2010.

Shippler, David K. *The Rights of the People*. New York, NY: Knopf, 2011.

Thomas, Kenneth R., and Todd B. Tatelman. *The Powers to Regulate Commerce: Limits on Congressional Power*. Washington, DC: Congressional Research Service, 2005.

U.S. Department of State. "Governance and Rule of Law: Two Year Fast Facts on the U.S. Government's Work in Haiti." Retrieved August 21, 2012 (http://www.state.gov/s/hsc/rls/179739.htm).

Walker, Samuel. *Presidents and Civil Liberties from Wilson to Obama*. New York, NY: Cambridge University Press, 2012.

White, Lawrence H. "The Rule of Law or the Rule of Central Bankers?" Cato Institute. Retrieved August 20, 2012 (http://www.cato.org/sites/cato.org/files/serials/files/cato-journal/2010/11/cj30n3-3.pdf).

ABOUT THE AUTHOR

G. S. Prentzas has written more than two dozen books for young readers. He also writes articles on legal topics for Lawyers.com, LegalZoom.com, and other Web sites. He graduated from the University of North Carolina with an A.B with honors in English and a J.D. with honors.

PHOTO CREDITS

Cover, pp. 1, 3, 9, 29, 45, 63. 82 © iStockphoto.com/Gyi Nsea; pp. 4, 14–15, 74 © AP Images; p. 10 DEA Picture Library/De Agostini/Getty Images; pp. 16–17 Ariel Skelley/Blend Images/ Getty Images; pp. 20–21 Robyn Beck/AFP/Getty Images; p. 23 Jim Arbogast/Digital Vision/Getty Images; pp. 26, 30–31 MPI/ Archive Photos/Getty Images; pp. 34–35 The Bridgeman Art Library/Getty Images; pp. 38–39 Hulton Archive/Getty Images; pp. 42–43, 61 The Washington Post/Getty Images; pp. 46–47 Bloomberg/Getty Images; pp. 50–51 dc_slim/Shutterstock.com; pp. 54–55 Saul Loeb/AFP/Getty Images; p. 58 Tim Sloan/AFP/ Getty Images; pp. 66–67 Emmanuel Dunand/AFP/Getty Images; pp. 68–69 David Leeson/Image Works/Time & Life Pictures/ Getty Images; p. 71 Mario Villafuerte/Getty Images; pp. 78–79 Keystone/Hulton Archive/Getty Images; p. 83 John Moore/Getty Images; p. 85 McClatchy-Tribune/Getty Images; pp. 88–89 Ethan Miller/Getty Images; pp. 92–93 Stan Honda/AFP/Getty Images; page and text box border images © iStockphoto.com/Wayne Howard (crowd & flag), © iStockphoto.com/DHuss (U. S. Capitol building), © iStockphoto.com/Andrea Gingerich (faces).

Designer: Les Kanturek; Editor: Nicolas Croce; Photo Researcher: Marty Levick